FOLLOW ME

Englisch für Anfänger

Band C1
Das Arbeitsbuch zu B1
Unit 1—30

von
L. G. Alexander
Roy Kingsbury

Langenscheidt-Longman · München
BBC London

FOLLOW ME
ist ein Gemeinschaftsprojekt folgender Institutionen
Bayerischer Rundfunk (BR)
British Broadcasting Corporation (BBC)
Hessischer Rundfunk (HR)
Norddeutscher Rundfunk (NDR)
Westdeutscher Rundfunk (WDR)
Österreichischer Rundfunk (ORF)
Schweizer Fernsehen (SRG)
in Zusammenarbeit mit dem Deutschen Volkshochschul-Verband
und dem Rat für kulturelle Zusammenarbeit des Europarats (CCC).

Koordination:
Joe Hambrook (BBC)
Dr. Gerhard Vogel (NDR)
Dr. Horst G. Weise (BR)

Deutsche Bearbeitung:
Langenscheidt-Redaktion

Bildnachweis:
British Airways: S. 16
Collins Publishers: S. 23
Home Office Immigration and Nationality Dept: S. 21

Umschlag:
Atelier für Werbegestaltung Wolfgang Rollmann

© *1979 BBC English by Radio and Television*
Deutsche Bearbeitung: © *1979 Langenscheidt-Longman GmbH, München.*
In Zusammenarbeit mit der TR-Verlagsunion GmbH, München.
Nach dem Urheberrechtsgesetz vom 9. September 1965 i. d. F. vom 10. November 1972 ist die Vervielfältigung oder Übertragung urheberrechtlich geschützter Werke, also auch der Texte, Illustrationen und Graphiken dieses Buches — mit Ausnahme der in §§ 53, 54 UrhG ausdrücklich genannten Sonderfälle — nicht gestattet.

Druck: Druckerei Appl, Wemding
Printed in Germany · ISBN 3-468-49805-5

UNIT 1 What's your name?

1 Study and Practise

> Is your name /Jones/ ? — Yes, it is./No, it isn't. It's /Smith/.
> Are you /John White/ ? — Yes, I am./No, I'm not. I'm /Sam Smith/.
> (*Am Telefon*) Is that /John/ ? — Yes, it is./No, this is /Sam/.

Ergänzen Sie:

1 'Is your name Smith?' 'Yes, ...'

2 'Are you Mr Smith?' 'No, ... I'm John White.'

3 'Is your name Jones?' 'No, ... Smith.'

4 '............................ Mary Black?' 'No, I'm not. Sorry.'

5 'Is your telephone number 34657?' 'No, ... 34658.'

6 '............................ Mary?' 'No, sorry. This is Susan.'

7 'Excuse me. .... Black?' 'No, it isn't. .... Johnson.'

8 'Good morning. .... Mary Brown?' 'Yes, ...'

2 Transfer: Reading and Writing

Situation: Sie haben im Urlaub auf Mallorca einen Engländer kennengelernt, und er hat Ihnen auf einem Zettel seinen Namen und seine Telefonnummer aufgeschrieben, so daß Sie sich bei ihm melden können, wenn Sie mal in England sind. Lesen Sie, was er geschrieben hat, und schreiben Sie ihm auf einem anderen Zettel dasselbe über sich auf!

> George Robinson
> Home telephone number: 01-636-3089
> Office telephone number: 01-266-4848

UNIT 2 How are you?

1 Study and Practise

a | Is he ...? Yes, he is / No, he isn't.
   | Is she ...? Yes, she is / No, she isn't.

Ergänzen Sie:

1 'Is he your brother?' 'Yes, ... His name's Alan.'
2 '.......... his wife?' 'No, she isn't. .... his sister.'
3 'Who's that? .... your brother?' 'No, ... He's my father.'
4 'This is Bill. .... my brother. And this is Susan. .... my sister.'

b *Setzen Sie* his, her, my *oder* your *in diese Sätze ein:*

1 That's John White. And that's .... wife – Mrs White.
2 How do you do? I'm John Lewis. And this is .... daughter, Kathy.
3 'Is that .... brother?' 'Yes, that's my brother. .... name's Sam.'
4 That's Mary. And that's .... sister, Sue.
5 'Your initials, please.' '.......... initials? S.J.'

2 Transfer: Reading and Writing
Situation: Sie sind zu Besuch bei einem englischen Bekannten. Er wollte Ihnen Namen und Adresse eines Zahnarztes heraussuchen. Dies hat er Ihnen aufgeschrieben:

> Dentist: His name's Mr Green. His address is 16, Station Road. His telephone number is 621 4093.

Übung: Notieren Sie für einen englischen Bekannten, der bei Ihnen zu Besuch ist, auf englisch Namen, Adresse und Telefonnummer eines Zahnarztes und eines Arztes:

Dentist: ....

....

Doctor: ....

....

UNIT 3 Can you help me?

1 Study and Practise

a *Formulieren Sie diese Aufforderungen etwas höflicher! Sehen Sie sich das Beispiel an und tun Sie dann dasselbe mit den anderen Aufforderungen!*

Beispiel: Wait here.
Sie schreiben:
    i) Please wait here.
    ii) Will you please wait here?
    iii) Would you wait here, please?

'MY NAME'S ZCHYSCHVESKIEVSKI. SHALL I SPELL IT FOR YOU?'

1 Come in. i) ....
   ii) .... iii) ....

2 Sign here. i) .... ii) ....
   iii) ....

3 Spell it. i) .... ii) ....
   iii) ....

b *can und can't*

Sehen Sie sich das Beispiel an und beantworten Sie dann die anderen Fragen schriftlich!
    Sie schreiben:

Beispiel: Can we park here? **PARKING** Yes, we can park here.
    It says 'Parking'.

1 Can we go in? **OPEN** 1 ....

2 Can I smoke here? **NO SMOKING** 2 ....

3 Can we go out that way? **ENTRANCE** 3 ....

4 Can we go in? **CLOSED** 4 ....

2 Transfer: Writing

Situation: Ein englischer Bekannter ist bei Ihnen zu Besuch und möchte wissen, was einige Schilder in diesem Land bedeuten. Suchen Sie fünf aus, skizzieren Sie sie und schreiben Sie zu jedem auf englisch, was es bedeutet! (Benutzen Sie, wenn Sie wollen, ein Wörterbuch!)

UNIT 4   Left, right, straight ahead

1 Study and Practise

a *Sehen Sie sich noch einmal den Plan an und wiederholen Sie die Verhältniswörter (3.1) auf Seite 15 des Lehrbuchs! Ergänzen Sie dann folgende Sätze zu diesem Plan und benutzen Sie dabei die angegebenen Verhältniswörter!*

1 The post office .... (*in*)
2 The police station ....
  .... (*on the corner of*)
3 The hospital .... (*at the end of*)
4 Barclays Bank .... (*near*)
5 The Grand Hotel .... (*next to*)

b *Schreiben Sie diese Sätze auf und benutzen Sie dabei die Kurzformen, die Sie in Unit 1–4 gelernt haben –* there's *für* there is, it's *für* it is *usw.!*

1 *Who is* that? *That is* Mary. ....
2 *How is* your wife? *She is* fine, thanks. ....
3 *Where is* the bank? *It is not* that way. ....
4 *I am not* John. *I am* Sam. ....
5 *There is* a hotel in West Street. ....

2 Transfer: Reading and Writing

Situation: Sie sind zu Besuch in England und wollen allein Winchester besuchen. Ein englischer Bekannter hat Ihnen diesen Plan von der Innenstadt gegeben und Ihnen folgendes über die Sehenswürdigkeiten aufgeschrieben:

① The Cathedral is in Market Lane. That's near The Square.
② The museum is in The Square, near the Cathedral.
③ King Alfred's Statue is at the end of The Broadway.
④ The Abbey House and Gardens are at the end of The Broadway, near King Alfred's Statue.

Tun Sie jetzt dasselbe für einen englischsprechenden Bekannten, der Sie in Ihrer oder einer anderen Stadt, die Sie gut kennen, besucht! Kennzeichnen Sie auf einem Plan oder einer Skizze Sehenswürdigkeiten mit einem Kreis, numerieren Sie sie und schreiben Sie kurz auf, wo sie sind!

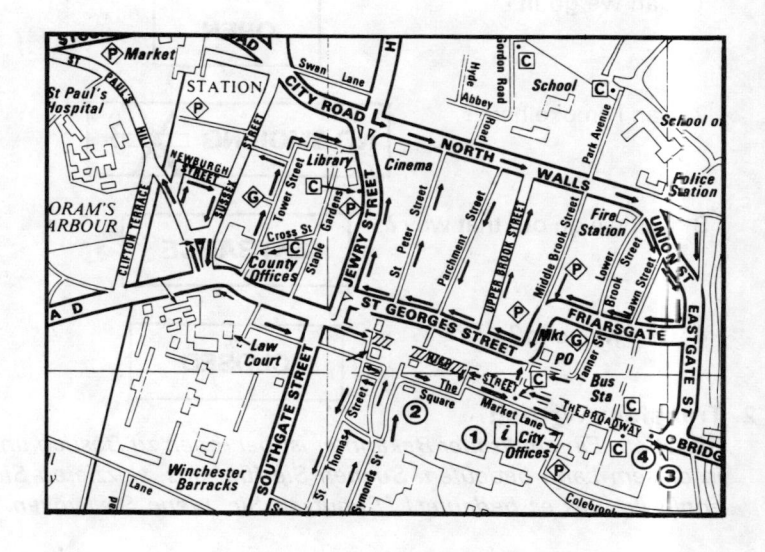

UNIT 5   Where are they?

1 Study and Practise

a *Sehen Sie sich noch einmal die Zusammenfassung (S. 20 des Lehrbuchs) und folgende Absätze in der Unit an:*

1.2 (p.17)	He's **at** the cinema.	*usw.*
2.2 (p.18)	He's **in** the kitchen.	*usw.*
3.1 (p.19)	He's **gone to** the doctor's.	*usw.*

Setzen Sie jetzt at, in *oder* to *in diese Sätze ein:*

1 Francis is ..... home. He isn't ..... his office.
2 She isn't ..... the garden. She's ..... the doctor's.
3 They're ..... Paris. They aren't ..... London.
4 John isn't ..... the cinema. I think he's ..... the theatre.
5 Mr Jones isn't ..... Hamburg. He's gone ..... Frankfurt.

b *Lesen Sie diesen Ausschnitt aus einem Brief und füllen Sie die Lücken aus:*

We are here ..... the National Hotel ..... London. It's ..... Victoria Station. There's a post office next ..... the hotel, and a theatre ..... the corner ..... the street.
Mary has gone ..... the shops (of course!), and George and Jane ..... gone ..... Buckingham Palace. And Sam has ..... to the Tower of London.

2 Transfer: Reading and Writing
Lesen Sie aufmerksam diese Postkarte! Stellen Sie sich vor, Sie sind im Urlaub und schreiben eine ähnliche Postkarte an einen oder mehrere Freunde in England oder den USA! (Achten Sie besonders auf die englische Schreibweise der Adresse!)

Hello! We are here on holiday at the Royal Hotel in Paris. I'm in my hotel room. Jim is at the National Museum and Susan has gone to Versailles.
Mary

Mr. G. H. Gordon,
14, Thomson Road,
BIRMINGHAM,
England

(five) 5

UNIT 6   What's the time?

1 Study and Practise

a

AT
We open **at** 9 o'clock. We close **at** 5.30.

ON
We're open **on** Mondays, Wednesdays and Fridays. We're closed **on** Tuesdays, Thursdays, Saturdays and Sundays.

Hier geht es um Öffnungszeiten von Geschäften und Banken in England. Setzen Sie at *oder* on *ein:*

Shops open . . . . 9.00 every day and close . . . . 5.30 or 6 o'clock. They are closed . . . . Sundays, and . . . . Wednesday or Saturday afternoons.
The banks open . . . . 9.30 every morning and close . . . . 3.30, but they are closed . . . . Saturdays and Sundays.

Schreiben Sie jetzt ebenso über Öffnungszeiten von Geschäften und Banken in Ihrem Land!

b *Sie sind in London. Sehen Sie sich den Fahrplan und das Beispiel an und schreiben Sie dann Sätze mit den angegebenen Zeiten:*

TRAINS TO SOUTHAMPTON				
London Waterloo	8.30	8.46	9.30	9.46
Winchester	——	9.53	——	10.52
Southampton	9.40	10.12	10.40	11.11

Beispiel: (It's 8.25.)
Sie schreiben: The next train will leave at 8.30 and will arrive in Southampton at 9.40.

1 (It's 8.40.) . . . .
. . . .
2 (It's 9.20.) . . . .
. . . .
3 (It's 9.35.) . . . .
. . . .

2 Transfer: Reading and Writing

Situation: Eine englischsprechende Bekannte oder Kollegin kommt nächste Woche in dieses Land. Hier ein Ausschnitt aus dem Brief, den Sie gerade bekommen haben und in dem sie Einzelheiten über ihre Reise mitteilt. Lesen Sie aufmerksam:

> My plane — it's LH 063 — will leave London Heathrow at 09.45 on Wednesday. I will arrive in Stuttgart at 11.15.
> Can you please meet me at the airport?

Sie fliegen nächste Woche nach England oder in die USA, um einen Bekannten oder Kollegen zu besuchen. Schreiben Sie ihm einen ähnlichen Ausschnitt aus einem Brief!

UNIT 7 What's this? What's that?

1 Study and Practise

a

this	hotel	bank	church
	river	shop	house
	tree	street	office
that	road	park	toothbrush
	bottle	cigarette	sandwich
	[z]	[s]	[ɪz]
these	hotels	banks	churches
	rivers	shops	houses
	trees	streets	offices
those	roads	parks	toothbrushes
	bottles	cigarettes	sandwiches

'AND WHAT'S THIS?'

Ergänzen Sie:

this *oder* these?
1 Is .... your toothbrush?
2 .... sandwiches are good.
3 .... is my office.
4 .... is West Street.
5 .... shops close at 7 o'clock.

that *oder* those?
6 .... churches are old.
7 Is .... your cigarette?
8 Who is .... over there?
9 There's a car park near .... houses.
10 .... offices are new.

b *Welche Antwort gehört zu welcher Frage?*

1 How old is that church?
2 How long is this street?
3 How heavy are those suitcases?
4 What colour are her shoes?
5 How high is this mountain?

a Two kilometres.
b 4,000 metres.
c White.
d About 500 years.
e About 20 kilos.

2 Transfer: Reading and Writing

Lesen Sie die Postkarte! Dann stellen Sie sich vor, Sie sind im Urlaub und schreiben eine ähnliche Karte über eine Sehenswürdigkeit an einen Bekannten in England oder in den USA. (Achten Sie wieder auf die englische Schreibweise der Adresse!)

Hello! We are here in Paris. This is a picture of the Eiffel Tower. It's about 350 metres high, and about 80 years old. See you on Saturday.
Peter

Miss W. Good,
20, Station Road,
BRISTOL,
England
(Angleterre)

(seven) 7

UNIT 8 I like it very much

1 Study and Practise

a like *und* don't like (+ quite, very much, at all); it *und* them

	Do you like **this wine**?	Do you like **those houses**?
+	Yes, I quite like **it**.	Yes, I quite like **them**.
+	Yes, I like **it**. *oder* Yes, I do.	Yes, I like **them**. *oder* Yes, I do.
+	Yes, I like **it** very much.	Yes, I like **them** very much.
–	No, I don't like **it** (very) much.	No, I don't like **them** (very) much.
–	No, I don't like **it**. *oder* No, I don't.	No, I don't like **them**. *oder* No, I don't.
–	No, I don't like **it** at all.	No, I don't like **them** at all.

Schreiben Sie Antworten zu den Fragen und sagen Sie, wie sehr Sie etwas mögen oder nicht mögen:

1 Do you like red wine?
2 Do you like old films?
3 Do you like the /Grand/ Cinema?
4 Do you like pop music?
5 Do you like airports?
6 Do you like old churches?
7 Do you like cheese?
8 Do you like this book?

b | Which do you prefer – tea **or** coffee? | I prefer tea **to** coffee. |

Setzen Sie to *oder* or *ein:*

1 I prefer Bach . . . Beethoven.
2 Which do you prefer – this book . . . that one?
3 I prefer your old office . . . your new office.
4 Who do you prefer – Jane . . . Mary?
5 I prefer small hotels . . . big hotels.

2 Transfer: Reading and Writing

Lesen Sie jede Aussage in diesem Fragebogen und haken Sie ab (✓), ob Sie zustimmen (+), keine Antwort wissen oder keine feste Meinung haben (?) oder nicht zustimmen (–)!

A QUESTIONNAIRE: WHAT DO YOU LIKE?	+	?	–	
1 I like Beethoven very much.				1
2 I don't like beer at all.				2
3 I prefer a Mercedes to an Audi.				3
4 I don't like parties much.				4
5 I like London very much.				5
6 I prefer Italian food to French food.				6
7 I quite like big hotels.				7
8 I don't like black coffee at all.				8
9 I prefer white wine to red wine.				9
10 I like French films.				10

Schreiben Sie jetzt auf, was Sie wirklich mögen, nicht mögen und lieber mögen!
Beispiel: I don't like Beethoven at all. I like pop music.

UNIT 9 Have you got any wine?

1 Study and Practise

a

I have (I've) got He/She has (He's/She's) got We/You/They have got (We've/You've/They've got)	a new radio. **some** cheese sandwiches. **some** German wine.
Has he/she got Have you/we/they got	a new radio? **any** cheese sandwiches? **any** German wine?
I haven't got He/She hasn't got We/You/They haven't got	a new radio. **any** cheese sandwiches. **any** German wine.

Setzen Sie has got, hasn't got, have got *oder* haven't got *ein:*

1 We . . . . . . some French mustard.
2 . . . she . . . a new dress?
3 He . . . . . . any suitcases.
4 They . . . . . . some good wine.
5 . . . you . . . any steak?

Setzen Sie some *oder* any *ein:*

1 Have you got . . . fresh fish?
2 We've got . . . French wine.
3 I haven't got . . . beer. I'm sorry.
4 Has she got . . . sandwiches?
5 He hasn't got . . . brothers.

b

There is/There's **some**	wine	here.
Is there **any**	cheese	there?
There isn't **any**	salad	here.

There are **some**	hotels	near here.
Are there **any**	cinemas	near here?
There aren't **any**	churches	near here.

Setzen Sie some *oder* any *ein:*

1 Is there . . . fish on the menu?
2 There aren't . . . parks in the town.
3 There are . . . magazines here.
4 There's . . . salt on the table.
5 There isn't . . . wine on the menu.

Setzen Sie there is, there isn't, there are, there aren't, is there? *oder* are there? *ein:*

1 . . . . any newspapers there?
2 . . . . any mustard on the table.
3 . . . . any French mustard?
4 . . . . some good restaurants near here.
5 . . . . any cinemas in the town.

2 Transfer: Reading and Writing

Dies ist ein Ausschnitt aus einem Brief von einem englischen Bekannten, in dem /er/ etwas über /seine/ Heimatstadt berichtet. Lesen Sie ihn aufmerksam und schreiben Sie dann ebenso einen Absatz über Ihre Heimatstadt, als ob Sie an einen englischen Bekannten schreiben würden.

> We've got some nice shops in the town and there are two or three good restaurants. There's "The Market Restaurant" near the station: I like that one very much. There aren't any theatres in the town, but we've got two cinemas. We've got two churches, and there's one hotel. It's the "Market Hotel" and it's about 400 years old.

UNIT 10 What are they doing?

1 Study and Practise

a Where are they?
What are they doing?

a) Mary is in the kitchen.
   She's making coffee.
b) John and Susan are at home.
   They're watching television.

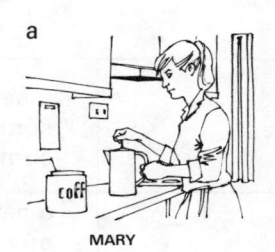

MARY

JOHN AND SUSAN

Schreiben Sie jetzt ebensolche Sätze über diese Leute:

1 JOHN   2 JANE   3 MR AND MRS SMITH   4 BILL

b

I	always never	drink tea at 6 o'clock. watch TV on Sundays. have a bath at 7.30.

He She	always never	drink**s** tea at 6 o'clock. watch**es** TV on Sundays. ha**s** a bath at 7.30.

Setzen Sie hier die richtige Form des Zeitworts (z.B. drink *oder* drinks) *ein:*

1 I always .... an apple every morning. (*eat*)
2 Mary never .... television. She doesn't like it. (*watch*)
3 Jane and her mother and father always .... to the theatre on Saturday. (*go*)
4 That man .... steak every day! (*eat*)
5 Jane never .... coffee. (*drink*)
6 John always .... his father on Saturdays. (*help*)
7 I never .... at home on Saturdays. (*stay*)
8 She .... to music every evening. (*listen*)

2 Transfer: Reading and Writing

Dies ist ein Ausschnitt aus einem Brief von einem englischsprechenden Bekannten, der einen kurzen Urlaub in London verbringt. Lesen Sie aufmerksam und schreiben Sie dann einen ähnlichen Abschnitt von einem Ort, den Sie gut kennen!

This is our fifth day here in London. Tomorrow morning we're going to the shops in Oxford Street. Tomorrow afternoon we're going to the Tower of London, and then tomorrow evening we're having a meal at a French restaurant.
We're going home the day after tomorrow.

UNIT 11   Can I have your name, please?

1 Names and Colours

Eine Reihe englischer Familiennamen sind Farbbezeichnungen. Wiederholen Sie die englischen Farbbezeichnungen (Unit 7, Lehrbuch, S. 27) und lösen Sie dann dieses einfache Rätsel! Setzen Sie mit Hilfe der Hinweise rechts die Namen der Leute ein, die in den übrigen Häusern der North Street wohnen!

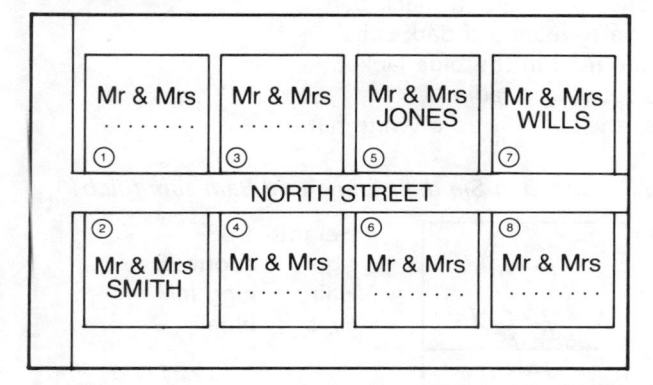

Mr & Mrs .... ①	Mr & Mrs .... ③	Mr & Mrs JONES ⑤	Mr & Mrs WILLS ⑦
NORTH STREET			
② Mr & Mrs SMITH	④ Mr & Mrs	⑥ Mr & Mrs	⑧ Mr & Mrs ....

Speech bubble: AND THE WINNING NUMBER IS DOUBLE TWO, DOUBLE NINE, DOUBLE THREE, DOUBLE SIX, DOUBLE SEVEN, OH, ONE.

LOTTERY N° 2289933667700

Lösungshinweise

1 Black + white = ?
3 Not white.
4 Red + green = ?
6 Not black.
8 Grass is this colour.

2 Transfer: Reading and Writing

a *Lesen Sie die Notiz und schreiben Sie dann nach den Angaben ähnliche Notizen!*

Notiz:
Mr. Smith is not here.
He's gone to the garage.
He's getting some petrol.
He will be here at 10:30.

1	2	3
Miss Wills the Market Restaurant having a meal 2.30	Mr Bass the car park parking his car 11.15	Miss Booth town getting some coffee 9.45

b *Situation: Während eines kurzen Urlaubs in einem englischsprachigen Land kaufen Sie etwas, das Ihnen in Ihr Land nachgeschickt werden soll. Die Verkäuferin hat Ihnen dieses Formular gegeben. Lesen Sie es und füllen Sie es aus!*

N & F Stores

Surname (Mr/Mrs/Miss)	
First Name(s)	
Road	
Town, Postcode	
Country	
Telephone Private	Business

UNIT 12 What does she look like?

1 Study and Practise

a

IN

> Mr Jones **is wearing** a brown suit.
> He's the man **in** the brown suit.
> The man **in** the brown suit is Mr Jones.

WITH

> Mrs Wilkins **is carrying** a parcel.
> She's the woman **with** the parcel.
> The woman **with** the parcel is Mrs Wilkins.

Setzen Sie in *oder* with, wearing *oder* carrying *ein:*

1 Is Jane the girl with the black bag? Yes, she's .... a black bag.
2 Is John the man .... the dark suit? Yes, he's wearing a dark suit.
3 Is Alan .... a blue jacket? Yes, he's the man in the blue jacket.
4 Is John the boy .... the radio? Yes, he's carrying a radio.
5 Is Mary the woman in the white hat? Yes, she's .... a white hat.

b *Lesen Sie diese Beschreibung von George. Beschreiben Sie dann Jane und Sam schriftlich!*

GEORGE

What does
George look like?
He is quite tall.
He is 1 metre 80.
He's 35 years old.
He's got short
brown hair and
green eyes.

Height: 1.80
Age: 35
Hair: short brown
Eyes: green

JANE

Height: 1.63
Age: about 25
Hair: long fair
Eyes: blue

SAM

Height: about 1.75
Age: 38
Hair: short dark
Eyes: brown

2 Transfer: Reading and Writing

Situation: Englische Bekannte haben Sie gebeten, einen jungen Mann bei sich aufzunehmen, der Ihre Sprache studiert. Sie haben sich einverstanden erklärt, daß er einen Monat bei Ihnen wohnen kann. Hier ein Ausschnitt aus einem Brief der englischen Familie:

> Our friend's name is Alan Blake. His address is 356, High Street, Bristol. (That's near our house.) His telephone number is Bristol (0272) 33667899.
> Alan is 20 years old and is about 1.70 metres tall. He's got short dark hair and brown eyes. He's a very nice young man. We think you'll like him.

Schreiben Sie einen ähnlichen Abschnitt über eine(n) junge(n) Bekannte(n) von Ihnen, der oder die bei einer Familie in den USA wohnen möchte!

UNIT 13   No Smoking

1 Study and Practise

a (i) *Bitte um Erlaubnis*

| May / Can | I | put my briefcase here? |

(ii) *Aufforderung*

| Would / Will | you | follow me, please? |

(iii) *Angebot*

| Shall / Can | I | get you a taxi? |

(iv) *Vorschlag*

| Shall we | go to the cinema? |

Setzen Sie may, can, will, would *oder* shall *ein:*

1 .... you put your suitcase there, please?
2 .... we listen to the radio?
3 .... I sit here, please?
4 .... you come in, please?
5 .... I bring you the bill, sir?
6 .... you get me another glass of wine, please?
7 .... we go home?
8 .... I smoke here?

b *Beachten Sie in diesen Sätzen die Formen* me *und* you *nach* get, give *usw.:*

Aufforderung
Would you **get me** another drink?
Will you **give me** your address?

Angebot
Shall I **get you** another drink?
Can I **give you** my address?

Schreiben Sie auf, was Sie in diesen Situationen auf englisch sagen würden:
Beispiel: Sie möchten zahlen. Sie schreiben: Would you bring me the bill, please?

1 *Sie möchten eine saubere Tasse haben.* Would ...
2 *Sie bieten jemand den Pfeffer an:* Can ...
3 *Sie brauchen ein Taxi.* Will ...
4 *Sie bieten jemand ein Sandwich an.* Shall ...
5 *Sie bitten jemand um seine Adresse:* Would ...
6 *Sie bieten jemand Käse an.* Can ...

2 Transfer: Reading and Writing

Sehen Sie sich aufmerksam die beiden Beispiele an und beantworten Sie dann die Fragen zu den vier anderen Schildern!

Beispiele: (i) **NO SMOKING**

Can I smoke here?
Sie schreiben: No, I'm afraid you can't.
It says 'No Smoking'.

(ii) **ENTRANCE**

Can we go in there?
Yes, of course we can/may.
It says 'Entrance'.

1 **Ladies**

Can I go in there?

2 **PLEASE KEEP OFF THE GRASS**

Can we sit here?

3 **OPEN**

Can we go in this shop?

4 **PRIVATE! NO ENTRY**

May we go in there?

UNIT 14   It's on the first floor

1 Study and Practise
Sehen Sie sich dieses Haus an und beantworten Sie dann die Fragen!

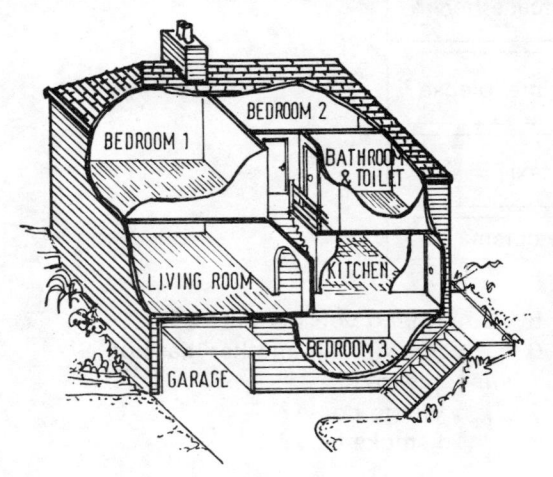

Beispiel: Where is bedroom 3?
Sie schreiben: Bedroom 3 is downstairs, on the ground floor, next to the garage.

1 Where is the kitchen?
2 Where is bedroom 2?
3 Where is the living-room?
4 Where is bedroom 1?
5 Where is the garage?
6 Where are the bathroom and toilet?

2 Transfer: Reading and Writing
Während Ihres Englandurlaubs haben Sie sich mit englischen Bekannten, die sich in Bath aufhalten, verabredet. Sehen Sie sich den Stadtplan an und die Beschreibung des Wegs zu Ihrem Hotel! Sie fahren von London nach Bath.

You are coming from London on the A4. And we are staying in a hotel in Bennett Street.
Go along the London Road into the Paragon.
Turn right into Landsdown Road and take the second turning on the left. That's Bennett Street.
The hotel is on the corner of Bennett Street and Russell Street.

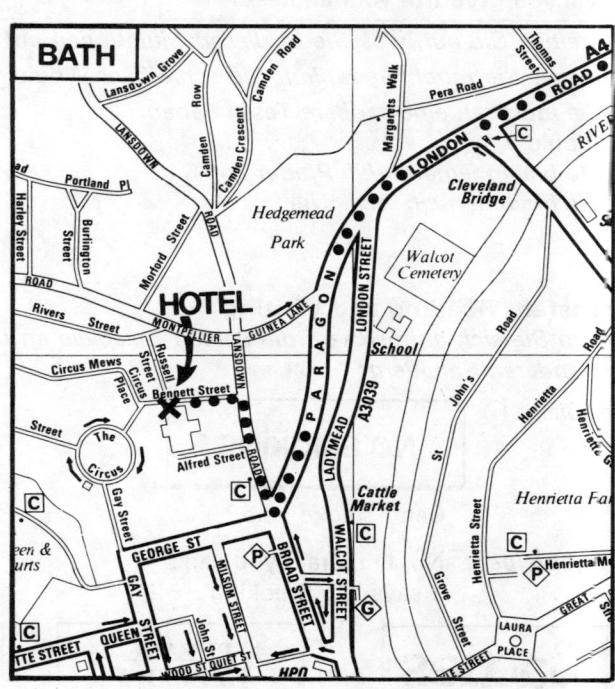

Tun Sie jetzt dasselbe für einen englischsprechenden Besucher, der mit dem Auto zu Ihnen nach Hause fährt. Zeichnen Sie den Weg in einen Plan Ihrer Stadt ein und geben Sie eine einfache schriftliche Beschreibung des Wegs!

UNIT 15 Where's he gone?

1 Study and Practise
gone *und* been

She isn't here. Where **has she gone**? She**'s gone** to town.	They aren't here. Where **have they gone**? They**'ve gone** to town.
Hello. Where **have you been**? I**'ve been** on holiday.	Ah, there they are. Where **have they been**? They**'ve been** on holiday.

Setzen Sie has gone, have gone, has been *oder* have been *ein*:

1 'There's George. Has he been to the cinema?' 'No, I don't think so. I think he . . . . . . to the theatre.'
2 I'm afraid Jill isn't here. She . . . to the shops. Can I take a message?
3 'You're brown. . . . you . . . on holiday?' 'Yes, I . . . . . . to Greece.'
4 'Is Mary there, please?' 'No, I'm sorry. She isn't here. She . . . . . . to the doctor's.'
5 'Is Mr Robinson in his office?' 'No, he isn't. He . . . . . . outside.'
6 Mr and Mrs Smith . . . . . . to lunch. They're coming back at three.
7 '. . . Bill . . . to the post office?' 'Yes, he has. He's in his office now.'
8 'Where's Mary?' 'She . . . . . . to the bank.'
9 'Where . . . Alan . . . ? I can't find him.' 'Oh, he's on the fourth floor.'
10 '. . . Jim . . . to the police station?' 'Yes, he has. Now he's gone to the car park. He's parking his car.'

2 Transfer: Reading and Writing

Diese Postkarte wurde von einem Engländer an ein englisches Ehepaar, das in Deutschland wohnt, geschrieben. Lesen Sie sie. Stellen Sie sich dann vor, Sie sind mit Ihrer Familie oder mit Bekannten im Urlaub und schreiben eine ähnliche Karte an einen Bekannten in England oder in den USA!

We're still here in London. We've been to Madame Tussauds and the Tower of London. And the boys have been to the British Museum. Jim's not here at the moment. He's gone to the Houses of Parliament with the boys.
Best wishes, P.

Mr. and Mrs. G. H. Jones,
Berlinerstrasse, 472,
D 3000 HANNOVER 83

FED. REP. GERMANY

UNIT 16 Going away

1 Study and Practise

a

ON	Friday(s) Saturday(s) weekdays	AT	weekends the weekend night	AT	9 o'clock 9.15 9.45	IN	the morning the afternoon the evening

Sehen Sie sich den Flugplan rechts und die Beispiele links an! Ergänzen Sie dann die übrigen Sätze unten mit Angaben aus dem Flugplan!

Beispiele:

There are flights to Moscow at 10.45 on Mondays, Fridays and Saturdays.
The plane leaves Heathrow Airport at 10.45 in the morning and arrives in Moscow at 4.20 in the afternoon.

LONDON—MOSCOW

DEPART London, Heathrow Airport. BE flights: Terminal 1 (Minimum check-in time at pier gate 20 mins)
BA flights: Terminal 3 (Minimum check-in time 60 mins, First class 45 mins)
SU flights: Terminal 2 (Minimum check-in time 60 mins)
ARRIVE Moscow, Sheremetievo Airport North

Frequency	Aircraft Dep	Arr	Via	Transfer Times	Flight	Aircraft	Class & Catering
Mo Fr Sa	1045	1620	non-stop		BE708	TRD	FY ✗
Tu Sa	1135	1710	non-stop		BA7	707	FY ✗
Fr Su	1155	1725	non-stop		SU581	IL6	FY ✗
Sa	1305	1835	non-stop		SU242	IL6	FY ✗
Tu Th Su	1350	1920	non-stop		SU242	IL6	FY ✗
We Fr	1450	2020	non-stop		SU242	IL6	FY ✗
Mo	2300	0430¹	non-stop		SU244	IL6	FY ✗

¹ — Next day

1 There are flights to Moscow . . . 11.35 . . . .

2 The plane leaves Heathrow Airport . . . 11.35 . . . .

. . . .

3 There are flights . . . . Wednesdays and Fridays.

4 The plane . . . .

. . . . 8.20 . . . .

b *Setzen Sie* was, wasn't, were *oder* weren't *ein:*

1 John and Mary . . . . late this morning. They . . . . early. 2 Sam . . . . at work yesterday. He . . . . at home. 3 We . . . . all late last night. We got home at 11.30. 4 I . . . . in London last week. I was in Paris. 5 Where . . . . you last night? I . . . . at the cinema.

2 Transfer: Reading and Writing

Situation: In diesem Ausschnitt aus einem Brief berichtet eine englischsprechende Bekannte über ihren Urlaub. Lesen Sie aufmerksam:

> The plane left Heathrow Airport at 11.30 in the morning. The flight was two hours late. We had a good flight and arrived in Rome at 3 o'clock in the afternoon. We were late, of course!

Schreiben Sie jetzt einen ähnlichen Ausschnitt aus einem Brief über Ihren letzten Urlaub oder eine Reise, die Sie vor kurzem mit Bahn, Flugzeug, Bus oder Schiff gemacht haben!

UNIT 17   Buying things

1 Study and Practise

a

Preis	How much is this/are these? How much does this/do these cost?	(It's/It costs They're/They cost) /£8.50/.
Material	What's it made of? What are they made of?	(It's They're) made of /nylon/.
Größe	What size is this hat? What size are these shoes?	(It's They're) /size 7/.
Für wen	Who is it for? Who are they for?	(It's They're) for /my wife/.

Sehen Sie sich die Bilder von Dingen an, die Sie für Mitglieder Ihrer Familie gekauft haben! Beschreiben Sie jedes kurz, wie im Beispiel, und sagen Sie, für wen es gedacht ist!

Beispiel: This shirt is made of nylon. It's size 15½ and it was £6.50p. It's for my brother.

b
It's **too big**. It's **not small enough**.	I'm looking for something **smaller**.

Ergänzen Sie die Sätze mit *too, not . . . enough* oder einem gesteigerten Eigenschaftswort (smaller, bigger usw.):

1 This hat is the wrong size, I'm afraid. It's . . . . big . . . .
2 This suitcase is too heavy. I'm looking for something . . . .
3 £100? That's . . . . expensive. I want something about £50.
4 These shoes are . . . . small. They're size 6, and my size is 7.
5 This radio is . . . . cheap . . . . I'm looking for something . . . .
6 This bag is . . . . good . . . . I'm looking for something made of leather.

2 Transfer: Writing

Lesen Sie den Ausschnitt aus einem Brief einer englischsprechenden Kollegin, die Sie in wenigen Tagen besuchen wollen! Beschreiben Sie dann in ähnlicher Weise einer Kollegin aus England oder den USA, die Sie besuchen kommt, was sie Ihnen mitbringen soll!

> Can you get a handbag for me, please? I'm looking for a black one, made of real leather. Not too expensive, please. I want to pay about £15.

UNIT 18 Why do you like it?

1 Study and Practise

> I'm looking for a quiet hotel. = I'm looking for a hotel **which** is quiet.
> I like/don't like quiet hotels. = I like/don't like hotels **which** are quiet.

In diesem Ausschnitt aus einem Brief von einem englischen Bekannten fehlt einiges. Lesen Sie und ergänzen Sie rechts die fehlenden Teile:

Schreiben Sie hier:

We're here on holiday in a hotel in Blackpool. It's a big hotel. I like it. But it's a very expensive hotel. I don't like that very much.

I like hotels which are big.
I don't like hotels which are very expensive.

And we've got a room without a shower. I don't like that.

I don't like ....
....

But the hotel is near the sea, and I like that.

I like ....
....

I've just got a new coat. It's made of fur and it's got buttons. I like it.

I like coats ....
....

Now I want a black bag – made of leather, and without a zip.

I'm looking for one ....
....

2 Transfer: Reading and Writing

Lesen Sie die Aussagen in diesem Fragebogen und haken Sie ab (✓), ob Sie jeweils mit A, B oder C einverstanden sind!

A QUESTIONNAIRE: WHAT DO YOU LIKE?		
A	**B**	**C**
1 I like dogs.	I like cats.	I don't like cats or dogs.
2 I don't like small hotels.	I don't like big hotels.	I don't like any hotels.
3 I prefer cats to dogs.	I prefer dogs to cats.	I prefer people to animals.
4 I like Italian food.	I like French food.	I don't like Italian or French food.

Schreiben Sie jetzt auf, was Sie mögen und nicht mögen, und begründen Sie es, zum Beispiel:
 I like cats because they don't make much noise.
oder: I don't like cats or dogs because they aren't very clean.

18 (eighteen)

UNIT 19   What do you need?

1 Study and Practise

I need/want He needs/wants	**a** new desk. **some** new chairs. **some** coffee.
Do you need/want Does he need/want	**a** new desk? **any** new chairs? **any** coffee?
I **don't** need/want He **doesn't** need/want	**a** new desk. **any** new chairs. **any** coffee.

I'd like	**a** salad. **some** peas. **some** wine.
Would you like	**a** salad? **some** peas? **some** wine?

Beachten Sie: Oft benutzt man some (*nicht* any) *in Fragen mit* Would you like ...? *Der Fragende erwartet dann die Antwort:* Yes, I'd like some ....

Setzen Sie some *oder* any *ein:*

1 I need ... new shoes.
2 Would you like ... mustard?
3 He doesn't want ... money.
4 She doesn't need ... new clothes.
5 I'd like ... fruit.
6 Does he want ... vegetables?
7 I don't need ... new shirts.
8 She needs ... sleep. She's tired.
9 Would you like ... potatoes?
10 I'd like ... steak.

2 Reading and Writing

Lesen Sie den Fragebogen und haken Sie ab (✓), was Sie wirklich brauchen oder was Sie gern haben möchten!

A QUESTIONNAIRE: Which do you need?		Which would you like?	
some new clothes	☐		☐
some new shoes	☐		☐
a new coat	☐		☐
a holiday	☐		☐
a new job	☐		☐
a new radio	☐		☐

Schreiben Sie jetzt Sätze über das, was Sie brauchen oder gern hätten. Beispiele:

   I need some new clothes. I need a new coat and some shirts.
   I'd like some new clothes. I'd like a new coat and a hat.
oder: I'd like some new clothes, but I don't need any.

UNIT 20 I sometimes work late

1 Study and Practise/About you

> I always/usually/sometimes/often/never go out on Saturdays.
> *Beachten Sie:* I don't always/usually/often go out on Saturdays.

Ergänzen Sie die Sätze mit always, usually, sometimes, often *oder* never + *Wochentag (und Tageszeit) Ihren eigenen Gewohnheiten entsprechend!*

Beispiel: I . . . . . stay at home on . . . . . evenings.
Sie könnten schreiben: I always stay at home on Monday evenings.
            oder: I never stay at home on Saturday evenings.

1 I . . . . watch television on . . . . evenings.

2 I . . . . listen to the radio on . . . . mornings.

3 I . . . . work in the office on . . . .

4 I don't . . . . write letters on . . . . evenings.

5 I don't . . . . go to the shops on . . . . mornings.

2 Transfer: Reading and Writing

Dies ist ein Ausschnitt aus einem Brief eines englischsprechenden Freundes, der Ihnen zwei- oder dreimal im Jahr schreibt. Lesen Sie aufmerksam und schreiben Sie dann einen ähnlichen Abschnitt über einen kurzen Urlaub, den Sie vor nicht langer Zeit hatten!

> Last month Jill and I were very tired. We needed a short holiday. We often go to Brighton, and we went there. We left home on Friday afternoon and arrived in Brighton at 6 o'clock. We stayed at the London Hotel. It's a very quiet hotel. We like it very much. We had a good meal and played chess in the evening. On Saturday morning we walked along the beach. It was very nice. Then we looked at the shops and Jill bought a new coat. We went to the theatre on Saturday evening and watched a very good

Die Antworten zu einigen dieser Fragen werden Ihnen beim Schreiben helfen.

Where did you go? When?
Why did you go there?
Where did you stay? Did you like it?
Why/Why not?

What did you do there? What did you buy?
When did you come back home?
What did you bring home?

UNIT 21 Welcome to Britain

1 Study and Practise

What nationality are you?	(I'm) English.
Where are you from?	(I'm from) England.
Where do you come from?	(I come from) England.
Which town do you live in?	(I live in) London.
What's your job?/What do you do?	I'm a nurse/an engineer.
Where do you work?	(I work) in a shop/in an office.
Which languages do you speak?	(I speak) English and French.

Ergänzen Sie:

a Where *oder* What *oder* Which?
1 ...... do you work?
2 ...... do you do?
3 ...... do you come from?
4 ...... nationality are you?
5 ...... languages do you speak?

b in *oder* from?
1 I come ...... Italy.
2 Which town do you live ...... ?
3 I work ...... a restaurant.
4 Where are you ...... ?
5 I work ...... an office.

2 Transfer: Reading and Writing

a
Situation: Sie fliegen zum erstenmal nach England und bekommen im Flugzeug diese Landekarte für Besucher zum Ausfüllen vor der Landung. Lesen Sie sie aufmerksam und setzen Sie dann Ihre Personalien ein!

IMMIGRATION ACT 1971			LANDING CARD IS 28B		
Family name (in block letters) / Nom de famille en lettres majuscules / Familienname in Grossbuchstaben {					
Forenames / Prénoms / Vornamen {		Occupation / Profession / Beruf {			
Date and place of birth / Date et lieu de naissance / Geburtsdatum und Geburtsort {		Sex / Sexe / Geschlecht {			
Nationality / Nationalité / Staatsangehörigkeit {		Signature / Signature / Unterschrift {			
Full address in the United Kingdom / Adresse complete en Grande Bretagne / Volle Adresse in Grossbritannien {					
NR	FOR OFFICIAL USE RESERVE AUX SERVICES DE L'IMMIGRATION NUR FUR DEN DIENSTGEBRAUCH		V	BV	ST
ABR			IT	CS	DP

b
Schreiben Sie den ersten Absatz Ihres ersten Briefes an einen englischsprechenden Brieffreund. Nehmen Sie dieses Muster zu Hilfe:

My name is (*Ihr Vor- und Familienname*). I'm (*Ihr Alter*) and I am/am not married. I come from (*Ihr Land*) and I live in (*Ihr Wohnort*). I'm (*Ihr Beruf*) and I work in (*Ihre Arbeitsstelle*). I speak (*Sprache(n), die Sie sprechen*).

UNIT 22 Who's that?

1 Study and Practise

a

What nationality is he/she?	(He's/She's) English.
Where's he/she from?	(He's/She's from) England.
Where does he/she come from?	(He/She comes from) England.
Where does he/she live?	(He/She lives) in London.
What does he/she do?	She's a bank clerk/He's an engineer.
Where does he/she work?	(He/She works) in a bank/in an office.

Beantworten Sie diese Fragen nach Angaben aus der Personalkarte!

PERSONNEL RECORD CARD
SURNAME: Smith
FIRST NAME(S): Mary
ADDRESS: 35, London Rd, Dublin
NATIONALITY: Irish
OCCUPATION: Nurse
PLACE OF WORK: The Royal Hospital

Beispiel: Does she work in an office?
Sie schreiben: No, she doesn't work in an office. She works in a hospital.

1 Does she come from France?
2 What does she do? Is she a waitress?
3 Does she live in Belfast?
4 Is she German?
5 Does she work in a hairdresser's?

b

He **was / felt** ill yesterday. He had toothache. / a cold.

He **is / feels** ill today. He's got a headache. / a cold.

He **will be / will feel** fine tomorrow.

Setzen Sie feels, doesn't feel, felt, didn't feel *oder* will feel *ein:*

1 She .... very well yesterday, but she feels fine today.
2 He .... fine today, but he was ill yesterday.
3 Mary isn't well today, but I think she .... fine tomorrow.
4 'How's John today?' 'He .... very well, I'm afraid.'
5 Sam .... ill yesterday, but he'll be fine tomorrow.

2 Transfer: Reading and Writing

Lesen Sie diesen Teil eines Briefes, in dem der Schreiber jemand beschreibt, der in Ihr Land kommt und Sie gern besuchen möchte:

My friend's name is Mary Jones. She's about 25 years old. She comes from Ireland, but she lives in Bristol. She's a receptionist. She works in a big hotel in Bristol. She's a nice girl. She's about 1.75 metres tall, and she's got long black hair and blue eyes.

Schreiben Sie einen ähnlichen Abschnitt, in dem Sie einen Bekannten oder Verwandten beschreiben, der Bekannte von Ihnen in England oder in den USA besuchen möchte!

UNIT 23   What would you like to do?

1 Study and Practise

Beachten Sie: nach want, would like *und* have (to) *steht die Grundform des Zeitworts mit* to:
I want to play tennis.
I'd like to go out.
I have to stay at home.
Beachten Sie auch, daß alle drei für Handlungen in der Gegenwart und in der Zukunft gebraucht werden können.
Es ist höflicher, would like to *zu sagen (statt* want to).

"We'd like to take you, of course, but I'm sorry — you have to stay here."

Beantworten Sie jetzt die Fragen! Sehen Sie sich das Beispiel an!
Beispiel: What would you like to do this evening? (*watch TV/go out*)
Sie schreiben: I'd like to watch television, but I have to go out.

1 What would you like to do tomorrow? (*work in the garden/go to the office*)
  . . . .
2 Where would you like to go tonight? (*go to the cinema/stay at home*)
  . . . .
3 What would you like to do next weekend? (*go to the museum/stay in the office*)
  . . . .
4 Where would you like to go on Saturday? (*have a meal at Franco's/stay at home*)
  . . . .

2 Reading and Writing

Sehen Sie sich die Beispiele genau an und beantworten Sie dann die Fragen zu den übrigen Schildern schriftlich!

Beispiele: (i)

Can I turn right?
Sie schreiben: No, you can't.
You have to turn left.

(ii) **NO WAITING THIS SIDE**

Do I have to wait that side?
Yes, you do.
You can't wait this side.

1 **NO ENTRY. PLEASE PARK OUTSIDE**
Can I go in there?

2 **PLEASE LEAVE COATS HERE. DO NOT TAKE THEM INTO THE THEATRE.**
Do I have to leave my coat here?

3
Can I turn left or right?

4 **NO FREE PARKING
1 Hour: 10p
2 Hours: 15p**
Do I have to pay?

(twenty-three) 23

24 UNIT 24 How can we get there?

1 Study and Practise

How far is Bristol from London?	It's a long way from London. It's not very far from London.
How can I/we get to Bristol?	By bus/coach/car/plane/train/boat.

Ergänzen Sie:

a from *oder* by?
1 It's faster .... coach.
2 How far is it .... here?
3 They went to London .... car.
4 We're going there .... plane.
5 It's about 5 kilometres .... our house.
6 I always go to London .... train.

b How far *oder* How?
1 ..... can we get to the station from here?
2 ..... is it to the station from here?
3 ..... did you get here – by plane?
4 ..... is Paris from London?
5 ..... do we get to your house?
6 ..... is the nearest school from your house?

2 Transfer: Reading and Writing

Während Ihres Englandurlaubs haben Sie mit englischen Bekannten, die in Southampton wohnen, verabredet, sie zu besuchen. Sehen Sie sich die Karte und die Wegbeschreibung zu ihnen nach Hause an, die sie Ihnen geschickt haben! Sie kommen aus Winchester.

You are coming from Winchester by car on the A33. We live at 10, Kuyveton Road.

You come to a big roundabout. Go round the roundabout and drive down Bassett Avenue for about 1 kilometre. Then you come to another roundabout. Go round and drive along Winchester Road for about 1 kilometre. There's a roundabout there. Turn left into Hill Lane. Then Kuyveton Road is about 1 kilometre along on the right.

Tun Sie jetzt dasselbe für einen englischsprechenden Besucher, der zu Ihnen nach Hause oder zu einem Treffpunkt in Ihrer Stadt fährt! Zeichnen Sie den Weg auf einer Karte ein und beschreiben Sie ihn!

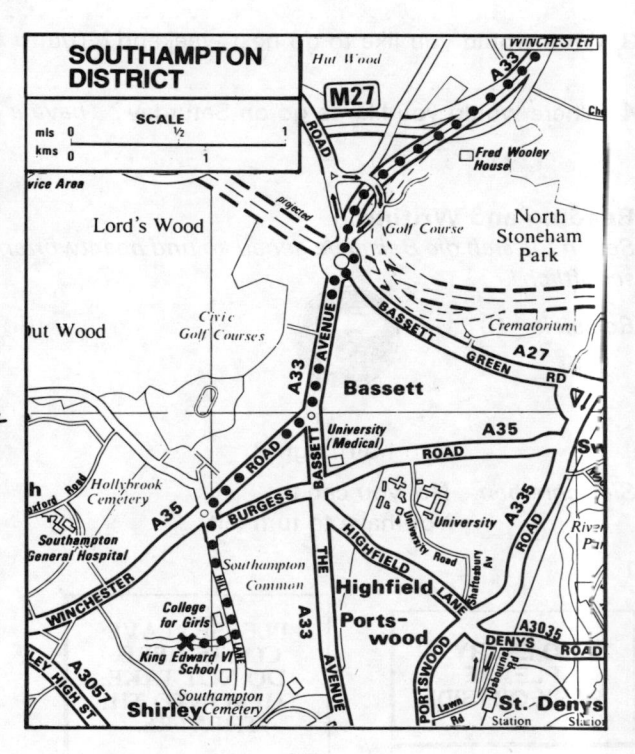

UNIT 25   Where is it?

1 Study and Practise
Dies sind die neuen Verhältniswörter, die Sie in dieser Unit gelernt haben:

Cambridge is **north of** London. The garage is **at** the front **of** the house. Cambridge is **between** Oxford and Newmarket.	You can go **through** the laundry room to the kitchen. The radio is **behind** the teapot. The saucers are **under** the shelf.

Setzen Sie of, at ... of, between, through, behind *oder* under *ein:*

1 The forks are in the drawer, ... the knives and the spoons.
2 You can get into the garden . . . . . . the back door.
3 Brighton is about 85 kilometres south . . . . . . London.
4 I think your shoes are . . . . . . your bed.
5 Our garage is . . . . the front . . . . our house.
6 'I can't find the sugar.' 'No, I'm sorry. It's there, ... the teapot.'
7 The small spoons are . . . . . the back . . . . . the drawer.
8 Reading is a town on the road . . . . . . London and Bristol.
9 It's about 65 kilometres west . . . . . . London.
10 You come in . . . . . . the front door and the kitchen door is in front of you.

2 Transfer: Reading and Writing
Sie wollen im Urlaub mit einer englischen Familie die Wohnung tauschen: Sie werden im Haus der englischen Familie wohnen und diese in Ihrem Haus. Hier ist ein Ausschnitt aus einem Brief, in dem die Engländer ihr Haus beschreiben. Lesen Sie ihn aufmerksam und teilen Sie ihnen dann in einem Brief das gleiche über Ihr Haus oder Ihre Wohnung mit!

> Our address is 94, Wimborne Road, Ferndown. (Our telephone number is 0202 394.) Ferndown is a very small town about 10 miles (16 kilometres) north of Bournemouth.
> Our house is about 20 years old and it's quite small. There's a living-room, small dining-room and kitchen downstairs. You come in through the front door and the living-room is on the right. (The stairs are in front of you.) The dining-room and kitchen are at the back of the house. Upstairs we've got three bedrooms and a bathroom, but two of the bedrooms are very small. Outside there is a big garden with a garage.

UNIT 26 What's the date?

1 Study and Practise

ON	Monday 13th March Monday, 13th March	IN	spring, summer, autumn, winter January, February, March, April, etc. 1956
How long will you be away? How long were you away?		(I'll be away) (I was away) FOR	two weeks. three months.
How long will the journey take? How long did the journey take?		(It'll take) a day. (It took) 3 hours.	*(Kein Verhältniswort nach take + Zeitangabe)*

a *Setzen Sie on, in, for oder – ein:*

1 We went to Austria .... 1971.
2 They're going away .... September.
3 He's coming home .... autumn.
4 We left .... 20th July.
5 The journey to London took .... 4 hours.
6 We went to Switzerland .... spring, 1955.
7 We left London .... 1st December.
8 They often have a holiday .... winter.
9 I was away .... 4 days.
10 My father's birthday is .... 2nd May.

b *Lesen Sie das Beispiel und schreiben Sie ebenso über die Pläne von Mary, Francis und Jane:*

Beispiel:
George
Go away: 7th July
Come back: 4th August
Be away: a month

Sie schreiben:
George is going away on 7th July
and is coming back on 4th August.
He will be away for a month.

1 Mary
Go away: 28th January
Come back: 4th February
Be away: a week

2 Francis
Go away: 20th May
Come back: 8th June
Be away: 3 weeks

3 Jane
Go away: 1st October
Come back: 30th November
Be away: 2 months

Schreiben Sie jetzt in der Vergangenheit über diese Leute:

Beispiel: George went away on 7th July and came back on 4th August. He was away for a month.

2 Transfer: Reading and Writing
In diesem kurzen Ausschnitt aus einem Brief schreibt ein englischsprechender Geschäftsfreund über seine bevorstehende Reise in Ihr Land. Lesen Sie ihn aufmerksam und schreiben Sie dann einen ähnlichen Abschnitt über einen Besuch, den Sie einem englischsprechenden Bekannten oder Kollegen abstatten wollen!

> I'm coming to your country next month. I'll be there on Monday, 20th April and I leave on Saturday, 25th April. I would like to come and see you on Thursday, 23rd April.

UNIT 27 Whose is it?

1 Study and Practise

Who's that man? That's Alan.

Whose	is that coat?
	are those shoes?
It's	mine / yours / his / hers /
They're	ours / yours / theirs.

Setzen Sie Who's, Whose, mine, yours, his, hers *usw. in die Sätze unten ein:*

1 That isn't my umbrella. .... is it?
2 Those bags belong to you. They're .....
3 Those suitcases are ..... They belong to me and Jim.
4 .... that girl over there?
5 I think that book belongs to me. Yes, it's .....
6 This radio belongs to Jane. It's ....
7 ... are these magazines?
8 These hats belong to Mary and Jane. They're .....
9 It belongs to you. It's .....
10 These leather suitcases belong to Francis. They're .....

2 Transfer: Reading and Writing

In diesem Briefausschnitt beschreibt ein englischsprechender Bekannter, der im Urlaub ist, sein Hotel und das Wetter. Lesen Sie aufmerksam und stellen Sie sich dann vor, Sie sind selbst im Urlaub und schreiben einen ähnlichen Abschnitt an einen oder mehrere Bekannte in England oder in den USA!

> The hotel is very nice. It's quite small and it's not far from the sea. The rooms are very nice too – they've all got a bath, television and telephone.
>
> The weather is very good. The sun's shining today and it's very hot – about 30°C. It's often foggy in the mornings and yesterday it was cloudy and it rained. But that's only one day in 2 weeks. (Last month it was very cold here and it snowed!)
>
> The weather forecast now is sunshine, sunshine, sunshine! What's the weather like in your country now?

UNIT 28 I enjoy it

1 Study and Practise

a
| I | enjoy/don't enjoy
like/don't like | **playing** tennis. |

| I enjoy/like **playing** tennis, but I prefer **watching** it. |

Ergänzen Sie die Sätze mit den angegebenen Wörtern:

1 I don't like .... things. (*make*)
2 I enjoy .... chess. (*play*)
3 Do you like .... football? (*watch*)
4 I don't enjoy .... to classical music. (*listen*)
5 'I like .... very much.' (*cook*)
  'Do you? I prefer ....!' (*eat*)
6 I like .... letters. (*write*)
7 They don't like .... at home. (*stay*)
8 I enjoy .... in the garden. (*work*)

b
| John's very **good** at tennis.
Bob **isn't** very **good** at tennis. |

| John plays tennis **well**.
Bob plays tennis **badly**. |

| John plays tennis **better** than Bob.
Bob plays tennis **worse** than John. |

Setzen Sie good, well, badly, better *oder* worse *ein:*

1 Jane's a good cook, but Mary cooks .... than Jane does.
2 Brian's very .... at tennis.
3 Francis isn't very .... at tennis.
4 John's a good driver. He drives very ....
5 George is a bad driver. He drives very ....
6 Peter plays tennis badly, but Francis plays .... than Peter!
7 That man speaks English very ....
8 Jane isn't very .... at spelling.
9 She can't spell very well. She spells very ....
10 That man's a good pianist. He plays the piano very ....

2 Transfer: Reading and Writing
Dies ist die Fortsetzung des Briefes über Alan Blake auf S. 12. Lesen Sie aufmerksam und schreiben Sie dann einen ähnlichen Abschnitt über einen jungen Bekannten, der als Gast bei einer Familie in den USA wohnen will!

> He enjoys going to the theatre and listening to classical music very much. Perhaps he can go to one or two concerts with you. He's good at tennis and would like to play on holiday. He plays chess very well too.
> He likes visiting museums and churches, and enjoys eating in restaurants. He enjoys Italian and French food.

UNIT 29 How many and how much?

1 Study and Practise

a

We've got some	biscuits tea	, but **only**	**a few.** **a little.**	///// 🍞
We haven't got	many biscuits. much tea.	We've got **very**	**few.** **little.**	///// 🍞

Setzen Sie a few *oder* a little, few *oder* little *ein:*

1 There are very .... potatoes here.
2 I've got only .... coffee.
3 They've got very .... milk.
4 There's only .... wine in the bottle.
5 We've got some steak, but only
  .....
6 There are only .... vegetables in this box.
7 We've got very .... luggage.
8 They've got some French francs, but only .....
9 She's got very .... clothes.
10 There's only .... milk.

b *Verbinden Sie die Begriffe aus Spalte A mit den richtigen Begriffen aus Spalte B und stellen Sie daraus eine Einkaufsliste zusammen:*

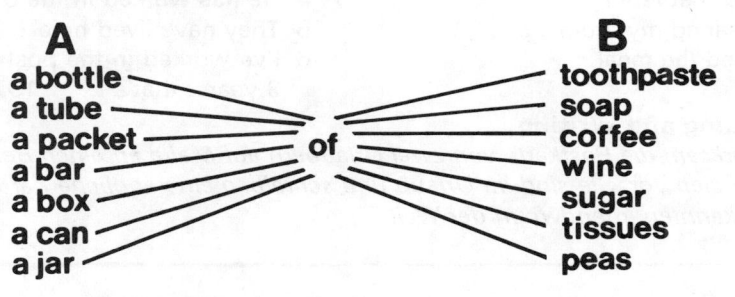

A
a bottle
a tube
a packet
a bar
a box
a can
a jar

of

B
toothpaste
soap
coffee
wine
sugar
tissues
peas

2 Transfer: Reading and Writing

Hier ist ein Ausschnitt aus einem Brief an den englischsprechenden Besitzer oder Hausmeister eines Ferienappartementhauses.

> We are arriving on Saturday, 5th August, at 9 o'clock in the evening. Of course, the shops will be closed. Would you please get these things for us:
> some potatoes; some bread; 2 cans of peas; 2 cans of fruit; a bottle of milk; some butter – just a little, enough for Sunday: 2 packets of biscuits; 1 packet of sugar; 1 packet of tea; a jar of coffee; some cold meat; and 2 bottles of wine.

Stellen Sie sich vor, Sie haben eine Ferienwohnung in einem englischsprachigen Teil der Welt gebucht! Schreiben Sie einen ähnlichen Briefausschnitt und sagen Sie dem Besitzer/Hausmeister, was er für Sie einkaufen soll für die Zeit, bis Sie selbst am Ort einkaufen können!

UNIT 30 What have you done?

1 Study and Practise

a
Have you written those letters **yet**?
(Yes), I have **just** written them.
       I have **already** written them.
(No), I have**n't** written them **yet**.
    (I'm still writing them.)

b
How long have you been a waiter?
I have been a waiter   **for 6 months.**
                             since 1st July.

'I SEE YOUR VISITORS HAVE GONE, MR SMITH. ARE THEY GOING TO COME AGAIN TOMORROW?'

Ergänzen Sie:

a just, yet *oder* not ... yet?
1 Have you done that work ....?
2 She has ... made some coffee.
3 I have ... been to the shops ....
4 Have you read that letter ...?
5 I have ... cleaned my room ....
6 I've ... cooked the meal.

b since *oder* for?
1 I've lived here .... 10 years.
2 She has worked here ... August.
3 I've been in London .... Saturday.
4 He has worked in the bank ... a year.
5 They have lived here .... 1969.
6 I've worked in the post office ....
   3 years: that's .... 1977.

2 Transfer: Reading and Writing

Lesen Sie aufmerksam die Postkarte von zwei Urlaubern auf Malta an einen Bekannten in England! Dann stellen Sie sich vor, Sie sind im Urlaub und schreiben eine ähnliche Karte an einen englischsprechenden Bekannten irgendwo in der Welt.

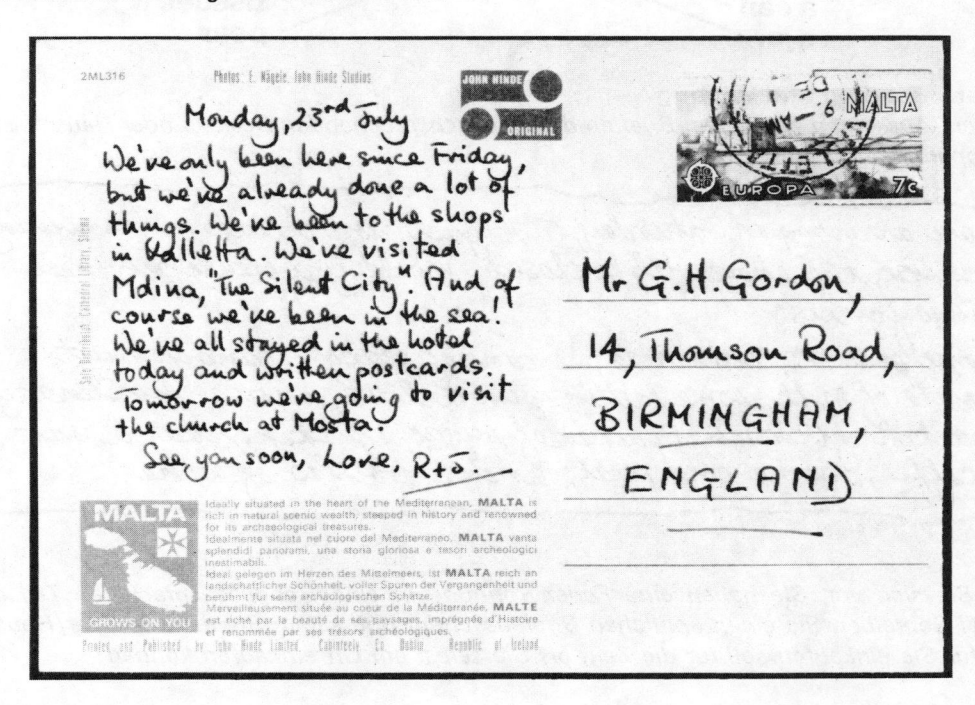

Monday, 23rd July

We've only been here since Friday, but we've already done a lot of things. We've been to the shops in Valletta. We've visited Mdina, "The Silent City". And of course we've been in the sea! We've all stayed in the hotel today and written postcards. Tomorrow we're going to visit the church at Mosta.
See you soon, Love, R + J.

Mr G. H. Gordon,
14, Thomson Road,
BIRMINGHAM,
ENGLAND